Mexican
Papercutting

MEXICAN PAPERCUTTING

Simple Techniques for Creating Colorful Cut-Paper Projects

◉ Banners ◉ Greeting Cards ◉ Masks
◉ Luminarias ◉ Table Runners & More

Kathleen Trenchard

DEDICATION
To my mother, Joanne Schwartz Williams, who
introduced me to the charm and versatility of paper cutting.

Editor: Deborah Morgenthal
Art Director and Production: Celia Naranjo
Photography: Evan Bracken
Production Assistance: Bobby Gold

Library of Congress Cataloging-in-Publication Data
Trenchard, Kathleen
    Mexican papercutting: simple techniques for creating colorful cut-
paper projects / Kathleen Trenchard.—1st ed.
        p.   cm.
    Includes index.
    1. Paper work—Mexico.   2. Folk art—Mexico.   I. Title.
  TT870.T7316 1997
  736'.98—dc21   97-22638
                                            CIP

Additional photography: Nancy Fullerton, page 26; San Francisco Craft & Folk Art Museum, pages 11 and 65;
Jon Thompson, pages 2, 9, 12 (lower right), 13 (top), 18 (top right), 19, 21 (top), 28-31, 33-35, 42, 45, 54-55, 56,
57, 67, 68, 69, 74, 76, 82, 85

10 9 8 7 6 5 4 3 2 1

First Edition

Published by Lark Books
50 College St.
Asheville, NC 28801, US

Distributed by Random House, Inc., in the United States, Canada, the United Kingdom, Europe,and Asia
Distributed in Australia by Capricorn Link (Australia) Pty Ltd., P.O. Box 6651, Baulkham Hills Business Centre, NSW
2153, Australia
Distributed in New Zealand by Tandem Press Ltd., 2 Rugby Rd., Birkenhead, Auckland, New Zealand

Table of Contents

Acknowledgments

To the many who have given generously of their knowledge, talent, and time in support of this publication, I am most grateful. I hope that the fine work of many artists, some unknown, will not go unnoticed, for they have contributed to a rich and vibrant tradition. Among the artists interviewed, Ernesto Vivanco and Victor Cuellar Fernandez must be singled out for their insight, enthusiasm, and patience. Additional expertise came from Judith Bronowski, Joseph Bean, and Manuel Salazar Riveroll.

For their help in providing materials from the Franz Mayer Collection, I am grateful to Eugenio Sisto, Lilia Rivera, and their staff. Erma Gomes was most generous with information from the McAllen International Museum. From the earliest stages of the writing, Dr. Marion Oettinger, San Antonio Museum of Art, Latin American Curator; Dr. Merle Wachter; and Stephen Vollmer all offered insight, information, commentary, and editing. Nancy Fullerton, world traveler and assistant curator at the San Antonio Museum of Art, has also been very generous with support and resources. Thanks also to the Roger Thayer Stone Center for Latin American Studies, and, especially, Linda Curcio Nagy. I am indebted as well to Peggy Day for her enthusiasm in sharing her knowledge and unique cut paper collection to enrich this book.

Deborah Morgenthal had the vision and task of organizing and enhancing the original manuscript and then editing the final version. Thanks also to Evan Bracken for his skill and patience in photographing the delicate works, and to Celia Naranjo for her talent and expertise in giving form and delight to the design of the book. And, of course, I very much appreciate Rob Pulleyn, publisher of Lark Books, for giving an enthusiastic thumbs-up to this undertaking.

Finally, I wish to acknowledge the devoted work of my photographer, computer expert, proofreader, traveling companion, and most patient and supportive husband, Jon Thompson.

Preface

I n an out-of-the-way niche in a San Antonio gallery, I noticed a cluster of delicately cut banners hanging in tiers of lavender, pink, and purple, all casting lacy shadows on the wall behind them. The lattice-like designs formed fanciful, even humorous skeletons, each enclosed within an elaborate border. Upon closer inspection, the work revealed itself to be intricate cuttings made of tissue paper. This, I was told was *papel picado*; and thus began my initiation and fascination with the ephemeral world of Mexican folk art.

I am not alone in my appreciation of papel picado. While working with art educator, Sylvia Orozco, I had the opportunity to observe and assist workshops in which participants experienced for themselves the particular thrill of cutting tissue paper, using traditional tools, techniques, and patterns. In preparation for later workshops on papel picado, I began researching the subject. As nothing was available in print, I was inspired to write a book combining the history of this folk art with patterns and project that crafters could re-create for their own enjoyment.

This collection of simple and more complex designs can be used for various occasions; simply reproduce them on a standard copier. Or, you may decide to use them as a springboard for your own experiments in pattern design. Once you have learned the basic methods, you can create new patterns using any kind of image you like. Whenever available, I have included traditional examples of papel picado to illustrate their modification for easy scissor cutting.

I could not resist adding a few ideas for further embellishment of cut paper that are not necessarily traditional to Mexico...yet. I encourage you to explore new materials, methods, and uses of cut paper. For instance, laser and die cutting are presently in use, but I have not included them here.

In addition to the 20 projects, the book features—for illustration and inspiration—dozens of examples of current and historical works of papel picado. Collectors and aficionados of folk art will, I hope, enjoy reading about the history and methods that have influenced Mexican paper cutting over the years.

The methods and materials I explain here have been used successfully in both informal and highly structured classroom settings, where time is often a major factor. Perhaps this book can also offer teachers a dynamic way to combine historical and cultural traditions with an easy, appealing hands-on activity.

Introduction

hen traveling through Mexico, one often finds streets and plazas decorated with strings of colorful cut-paper banners fluttering in the breeze. These ubiquitous decorations are known as *papel picado*, which is "punched paper" in Spanish. The term also describes the traditional folk art used in Mexico to decorate altars, tables, windows, ceilings, and plazas during festivals. Mexican artisans who produce papel picado use hammer and chisel to cut up to 50 layers of tissue paper at a single stroke. The size of these works ranges from diminutive three-by-five-inch (8 by 13 cm) flags to altar decorations over 36 feet (11 m) wide. It is traditional to use

tissue paper in the production of papel picado, but other materials, such as metallic foil, coated papers, reflective mylar, and plastic, are becoming commonplace.

Colorful, lacelike canopies announce holidays, such as All Souls' Day (*El Dia de Todos Santos*) and Day of the Dead (*El Dia de los Muertos*) on November 1 and 2. Secular occasions, ranging from the national Mexican Independence Day, on September 16, to the very local opening of a new street, are announced with cut banners crisscrossing the sky. In the state of Veracruz, Mexico, gray moss is interspersed with fluorescent cut-plastic banners. In time, the wind reduces the flags to tatters, but the moss thrives as a reminder of past festivities.

Larger, more detailed banners, resembling decorative curtains, can be seen gracing windows or doors. For religious occasions, cut paper is often draped over home altars and dinner tables. Letters and numbers are artfully cut into the paper announcing where and when a celebration will take place. Typical themes, such as birds and flowers, can vary from simple to elaborate works. Even the simplest papel picado, with geometric shapes cut into rectangular flags, lends gaiety and texture to an event.

Papel Picado banners hanging over a monastery plaza in Cholula, Puebla, in Mexico

Paper as an Ephemeral Art Medium

A living folk art, papel picado continues to evolve in Mexico, although its tools and execution have changed little during this century. Many of the themes and motifs found in papel picado are also found in other forms of Mexican folk art. Traditional designs used in Mexican lacquer work, painted pottery, metal work, and textiles have a striking similarity to the motifs and border patterns of papel picado. This imagery stems in part from earlier European, Moorish, Oriental, and native influences. A preference for specific design elements and themes evolved over the course of 400 years, as generations of Mexican artisans refined their techniques in service to patrons. The Mexican desire to embellish art and architecture can be appreciated in the country's earliest fine workmanship, as seen in the ancient sculpture and stone wall reliefs of pre-Colombian pyramids.

For most households, the "waste not" rule is simply a necessity of life; a family will recycle a product or use inexpensive materials to fashion simple decorations with inventive charm. Materials discarded or overlooked elsewhere, such as tin cans and oil drums, are transformed by Mexican folk artists into items as diverse as toy planes and food warmers. This embellishment of the ordinary extends to funerals and cemeteries, where wreaths are made more festive by using scrap-paper garlands. The relatively inexpensive colored tissue paper lends itself to formal yet ephemeral decorations.

As with other crafts, papel picado has become the specialty of generations of artisan families who satisfy the public demand for seasonal decorations. In this respect, papel picado has much in common with other forms of festive folk art—the *pinata* (also made of tissue paper), paper flowers, floral arches, and carpets, as well as edible art.

Once a festivity has ended, the paper banners are discarded or abandoned to the elements. It may seem ironic that so much time, labor, and creativity are invested in such a perishable material as paper. However,

This Mexican Independence Day banner is a good example of how separate sheets of tissue paper can be glued together.

Herminia Albarrán-Romero, who created the cut-paper altar work shown here, comes from a family of paper artists in Mexico. As a child she learned from her mother and father, who made paper decorations for their village church in San Francisco de Assisi, in Mexico. Her grandfather cut paper chains of vines, fruits, and bells that opened like fans. Herminia, who presently lives in San Francisco, California, is well known for her altar work. To walk into a space she has transformed into an altar with cut paper, paper flowers, offering breads, and other ritual items, is an inspiring experience. Although she works in a traditional manner and considers all of her work an offering (*ofrenda*) of devotion, she is a natural artist. She has been commissioned to make altars for the Day of the Dead by the San Francisco Arts Commission, the Berkeley Art Museum (University of California), the Oakland Museum, and the community-oriented Galeria de la Raza in San Francisco.

out of delicate materials, and rarely signed or dated by its creator, papel picado usually has a life span of less than a month. This anonymity and impermanence give a magic and spontaneity to an art that must be experienced firsthand to be appreciated fully.

However, artists are now finding that customers are willing to pay more for the more durable plastic banners, and, in Mexico, plastic of excellent quality is produced in an abundant selection of weights, colors, and sizes. From a distance one cannot distinguish between papel or *plastica picado*, except that the latter often takes the shape and color of

the use of cut paper for art work has a long-standing association with the ceremonial and spiritual. In Mexican and other cultures, ephemeral paper art is often a metaphor for human life—impermanent and transitional.

Produced in small family workshops for customers who buy it cheaply and use it immediately, papel picado is rarely seen far beyond the Mexican border, unless it has found its way to museums, galleries, or special events with a Mexican theme.

Even in Mexico, papel picado is either taken for granted or, in many areas of the country, totally unknown. Produced in large quantities

Florentino Reyonosa III is working with traditional tools in Huixcolotla, Mexico.

Plastic banners displayed over a car lot in Piedras Negros, Mexico to celebrate Mexican Independence Day

decorations associated with used-car lots and gas stations north of the border.

Papel picado is folk art produced within the tradition of a cottage industry. It is a vehicle of communication announcing sacred and secular messages. It is a commercial art form, yet it is handmade with skill, care, and imagination. There is a charm and grace in these paper cuts that will always transcend the mechanically produced decoration.

It has been enormously satisfying putting together this collection of papel picado. I hope you enjoy making your own cut-paper banners and other items, using the designs in this book. I hope, too, that you will be inspired to create your own designs. In this way, you will be participating in a unique and rich cultural heritage, so hard to find in the age of mass produced souvenirs and party props. Viva Mexico! Viva papel picado!

History of Cut Paper in Mexico

The history of papel picado is rich and varied. Its origins date back to the art of papermaking in pre-Colombian times. Its style has been influenced by the cultures of several countries, including China, Spain, and Germany. Since its beginnings, Mexican cut paper as been associated with spiritual rituals that commemorate death and the afterlife. Today, Mexican papercutting continues to serve as traditional embellishment for religious and ceremonial occasions. Its evolution as a contemporary folk art reflects the fascinating and complex society which inspires it. The reverent and the absurd are reflected in these cut-paper works; their charm and insight make them uniquely Mexican.

Pre-Columbian Origins

The origins of papel picado can be traced to pre-Columbian papermaking, which thrived throughout Meso America and survives into modern times in the regions of Puebla, Hidalgo, and Veracruz. Made from the pulp of the mulberry and fig trees, this ancient paper is called *amatl* by the natives. The process of drying, boiling, forming a grid with the pulp, and then pounding it into paper with large stones is strikingly similar to the methods and materials used by the Chinese as early as AD 105. Pre-Columbian rituals in which the dead were clothed in elaborate paper costumes parallel funerary customs still practiced in China, whereby possessions such as clothes and money

Otomi bark spirit figure from San Pablito, Mexico; Collection of Peggy Day

Horse snout amatl figure

Some spirit figures are still cut from amatl and sold in shops throughout Mexico. "Good spirits" are generally cut from the lighter-colored mulberry bark, while "evil spirits" are made of the darker fig bark. One of the latter is the "horse snout," (depicted above) which represents the spirit of a woman who did not show respect for her parents. She has a human body and the head of a horse and wanders about spreading disease and death.

Papel picado and amatl figures are both produced in the Sierra de Puebla and share similar borders and motifs. Often one or four amatl figures will be pressed into contrasting bark,

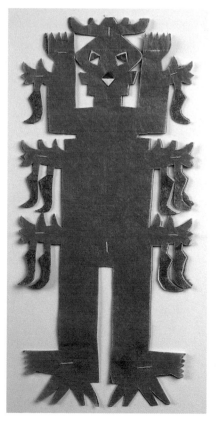

This Otomi spirit figure was made by stitching together contrasting sheets of colored tissue paper, and features some pop-up effects.

are reproduced in the less expensive paper for enjoyment in the afterlife.

Amatl, historically used for writing (codices) and as cut-paper spirit figures in pantheistic rituals, is now made in the remote village of San Pablito, Puebla, for commercial trade and the tourist market, and for paintings (made elsewhere) called "amates." With the availability of cheap commercially produced tissue paper (called *papel china* in Mexico), village shamans can now cut multiple layers of tissue with scissors to produce abundant spirit figures in bright colors to be burned during ritual offerings.

which serves as background and frame. Both papel picado and amatl figures are characterized by symmetrical organization and strong graphic qualities, highlighted with expression and intricacy. Recent amatl and even cut-tissue works from San Pablito reflect the influence of papel picado. The San Pablito pieces are usually smaller and are cut with scissors in small quantities.

The shamanistic use of paper cutouts survived Spanish Colonial Christianization only in remote mountain villages. With the arrival of the Spanish colonists in the 16th century, trade across the Pacific began. The Manila Galleon arrived annually in Acapulco from the Philippines, carrying exotic cargo that was then transported by mule overland to Veracruz and reloaded onto ships bound for Cadiz, Spain, to be distributed throughout Europe. This event was the occasion for several fairs throughout Mexico, especially along the routes connecting Acapulco and Veracruz, most notably Puebla and Queretaro.

Chinese Influence

Sixteenth-century Iberia was the child of Roman and Islamic traditions. Chinese art was translated by Moorish and eventually by Spanish artisans. With the European guild system intact in the city of Puebla, Mexicans could collect exquisite ceramic reproductions of Chinese and Spanish works by Mexican artisans.

The 17th- and 18th-century "medallion style" in Talavera ceramics from Puebla was directly influenced by Ming dynasty pottery. The "Talavera" style refers to the white lead coating over the clay, which is then fired twice.

Above, Chinese paper cut; opposite page, two Chinese-inspired stencils from Puebla

Stencils were often used to trace the design onto the pottery in preparation for painting. Some of the Chinese motifs seen on these "medallion style" ceramics, especially curly vines, birds, a variety of flowers, and the use of scalloped borders, are also used in traditional papel picado designs.

Puebla became the center of Talavera ceramics, and later of papel picado. Some similarity between Mexican and Chinese motifs may have begun with paper stencils imported into Mexico directly from China or through the Philippines. Made from water-resistant mulberry paper, these stencils were used by Chinese artisans as an aid in wood carving, textile

Both Chinese and Mexican paper-cutting traditions have been nurtured by peasants living in small villages. Similar bird and floral motifs are popular in both folk arts. In China, cut-paper banners are made to decorate door posts, windows, and ceilings as signs of prosperity and celebration. China and the Christian world both hold yearly festivals to encourage the remembrance of the dead. Cut-paper decorations and special edibles are prepared in China for this occasion and offered up to the spirits, later to be eaten by their descendants during a festival known as "Chung Yang."

dying, ceramic painting, lacquer ware, leather and metal working, and cotton appliqué. During Spanish Colonial times, Mexican craftsmen excelled in all of these trades, and Chinese paper stencils were plentiful and

inexpensive. In Puebla, packets of assorted colored-tissue (papel china) stencils, some with recognizable Chinese motifs, are still sold.

Buddhist streamers or colored flags are common features at Chinese funerals. Mexico honors its dead with much respect, humor, and festivity during the holiday of El Dia de los Muertos. Mexicans tend to favor white-tissue banners for funerals, but use color for most other occasions.

European and Religious Origins

Luis Vivanco, a renowned papel picado artist, believes that papel picado originated as altar decoration. Village churches with little money for lace chalice cloths found a substitute in cut-paper versions known as *cortinas*. Many altar coverings are still made of white paper. The overall background grid of horizontal and vertical connectors, which is unique to Mexican papel picado, compares in style and design with fine European lace designs of religious and secular figures. Dating back to the Baroque period, Spanish and Italian lace narratives, with lettering or captions enclosed in simple rectangular borders, can be found at the Victoria and Albert Museum in London.

Detail from *Chalice Cover*, 18th century, Mexico; paper, silk, gold and silver thread, 4¾" x 4¾"(12 x 12 cm) 87.63G; The Nelson A. Rockefeller Collection of Mexican Folk Art, San Antonio Museum of Art, San Antonio, Texas

This lacelike white tissue banner shows the pencil marks the artist drew to outline the design before cutting.

An intricate 18th-century cut-paper chalice cover (pall) from Mexico is included in the Rockefeller Collection at the San Antonio Museum of Art. It was a gift to Nelson Rocke-feller from Roberto Montenegro, an early pioneer of Mexican folk art. Less than five inches square, the piece simulates white lace and is mounted on salmon-colored silk. The composition is symmetrical except for the "Lamb of God" holding a banner in the center of the heart shape. The heart is formed by the same vine that blossoms into a flower and a butterfly and finally ends in clusters of grapes at each of the four corners of the square. Rather than the standard horizontal and vertical grid mentioned above, here the grapevine grows into an organic grid, which is seen in both European and Oriental paper cutting. The organic theme continues in the border, where a contrasting zigzag pattern is formed by what appears to be an elegant use of the vegetable, okra. The outer edge of this border is scalloped with tiny triangles, as if cut with tiny pinking shears.

Sacred Heart, 19th-century cut paper; 3" × 5" (7.5 × 13 cm). Museo Franz Mayer, Mexico City

When this tiny beauty is viewed under magnification, irregularities in the cutting of details, such as the larger holes and five-pointed stars, suggest the use of scissors. The scale, style, and content of the chalice cover bear comparison to some of the miniature 19th-century cut-paper works in the Museo Franz Mayer in Mexico City.

Who might have had the patience and skill to complete such painstaking work? Just as medieval monks dedicated countless hours to the scrolling and illustration of illuminated manuscripts, cloistered members of monastic orders may have spent many hours cutting paper holy cards and religious certificates. On the other hand, evidence of the popular Ger-man *scherenschnitte* tradition is apparent in the cutting of figures and landscape themes of a secular nature also found in the Mayer Collection.

Jewish Influence

Some of the intricate filigree seen in the above mentioned works resembles that used in traditional Jewish paper cuts, executed by folk artists as early as the 17th century. Like the Mexican miniature paper cuts, many Jewish examples also incorporate an organic grid with a religious text or inscription, which is actually cut paper calligraphy. Christian art of Spain and Mexico has been enriched by the intricate and symbolic influence of Jewish liturgical art. The Rockefeller chalice cover appears to be such an example.

A.L.M. Magdalena, detail of 19th-century cut-paper work, 3" × 5" (7.5 × 13 cm); Museo Franz Mayer, Mexico City

El Dia de los Muertos

Although Halloween has become a secular holiday in some parts of Mexico, the medieval European feasts, All Saints' Day and All Souls' Day, maintain a mystical significance for most Mexicans. In current practice, Mexicans honor the spirits of departed children on November 1 (*El Dia de los Angelitos*) and of departed adults on November 2, which is also the national holiday of the Day of the Dead. These two days are among the most important Mexican festivals, during which homemade altars are adorned with the favorite foods and personal items of those remembered. Much ephemeral art is produced for this occasion—skeleton toys, papier maché rockets in the shape of skeletons and devils, garbanzo bean funeral procession figures. Elaborate canopies, backdrops, table and altar coverings, all made of cut tissue paper, are a major ingredient in the festive and elegant decorations for this event.

Although pink, orange, white, and black are traditional Day of the Dead colors, a more inventive use of color seems to be a trend, as evidenced by the work of contemporary artists. Papel picado altars and installations produced for this occasion and for All Soul's Day incorporate skeleton and devil motifs, angels, and grave yard scenes, rendered in many distinctive colors.

It is in the tradition of the Day of the Dead that one begins to appreciate the rich synthesis of pre-Columbian and Christian cultures. The Aztec preoccupation with sacrificial death and skull imagery was matched by the pervasive

Papel picado inspired by a work by Jose Guadalupe
Posada; see discussion on page 22

Day of the Dead altar installation at the Mexican
Cultural Institute in San Antonio, Texas

European medieval concepts of *memento mori* and the *dance macabre*. In the hands of Flemish masters such as Hieronymus Bosch and Pieter Bruegel, the "triumph of death" theme was depicted with remarkable imaginative detail. Reproduced in woodcuts, these images were brought to the New World by Spanish missionaries, and have been tempered by modern Mexicans to reflect their stoicism and humor. The entire Day of the Dead festival embodies the question: "If life begins after death, why mourn the dead?" Papel picado designs made for the occasion feature playful, humorous, sometimes satirical portrayals of the dead and living—human, animal, and celestial—all depicted as skeletons. As the cut-paper images on these pages demonstrate, the medieval dance of death in contemporary Mexican culture continues to evolve and delight.

Jose Guadalupe Posada

In his many engravings, woodcuts, and lithographs, the late 19th-century artist from Aguascalientes, Jose Guadalupe Posada borrowed images from medieval "last judgment" scenes of the damned being shoved into a gaping

Good example of a horizontal/vertical grid combined with an organic grid; see discussion on page 49

The reminder of death theme appears to have continued into 19th-century Europe as well. A little known, mysterious collection of French photographs, dating from the mid-19th century, reveals elaborate tableaux of miniature skeletons and devils in earthly settings, depicting hell as a humorously morbid mirror of Parisian life. One is reminded of Dante's *Divine Comedy* but also of Posada's prints, in which clergy and statesmen alike are portrayed as skeletons bumbling through daily life.

Like the folk art made for El Dia de los Muertos, Posada's prints or broadsides (called *calaveras*, meaning skulls or skeletons) were sold inexpensively and in large quantities. This popular art form was as much a Dia de los Muertos tradition as other ephemeral seasonal necessities such as the *pan de muertos* (bread of the dead), sugar decorated skulls, dancing skeleton puppets, rattles in the shape of skulls or devils, and pop-up coffins. Intended as biting satire on the Mexican establishment, these lithographs often included humorous captions in the form of a mock epitaph.

Jose Guadalupe Posada's *Don Quixote* and a cut-paper version

mouth of hell. He translated memento mori themes into reflections of his contemporary Mexico, which spanned the *Porfiriato*, or the period of 1780 to 1910, during the domination of President Porfirio Diaz, and leading to the Mexican Revolution of 1910.

Today's papel picado artists in Mexico continue to be inspired by Posada. The woodcut technique, with its strong contrasts and bold designs, translates easily into cut paper. The faux lace cut-paper altarpiece (discussed above) became the appropriate format for El Dia de los Muertos and All Saints' Day imagery and decoration.

La Catrina

The most popular and famous of Posada's calavera stereotypes is "La Catrina," always dressed as a fashionable Victorian lady. La Catrina has become a common motif in Day of the Dead papel picado. She is easy to recognize as she flirts with her fan, dances and dines in her elegant long bustled skirt, with a skele-

Posada's *La Catrina* and a cut-paper rendition at right

tonlike waist, little lace purse, and huge plumed hat. Posada was perhaps paraphrasing a popular medieval theme once again, in this case the theme of vanity (one of the seven deadly sins), as a reminder that beauty is fleeting. La Catrina may also satirize the short-lived but influential period of French rule over Mexico or the later Porfiriada, with its preoc-

cupation with European fashion, a form of ephemeral art for the elite. Or is La Catrina the symbol of Mexico itself—smiling even in death and always dressed for the occasion, making the most of it? The elegant La Catrina has become, at the very least, the symbol of El Dia de los Muertos.

Huixcolotla, Puebla, Mexico

Huixcolotla is a small dusty village, boasting two modest churches without pews. It is located at the end of the line on an hour-long bus ride, outside the cosmopolitan city of Puebla, in the state of Puebla. The busy road to Huixcolotla is punctuated by open markets and mission church ruins. Upon arrival, one is likely to be approached by a friendly villager, eager to escort you to the studio of a papel picado artist. In fact, there is an undercurrent of competition among certain artists for potential customers.

Luis Vivanco uses a hammer and chisel to cut a mylar hanging ornament.

The renowned papel picado artist Luis Vivanco lived here before moving to Puebla. His nephew, Ernesto Vivanco, a youthful 50-something, learned the art from him. Although not a single example of his uncle's work survives, even in reproduction, the tradition was passed to Ernesto who in turn is teaching the technique of picando to his two sons and daughter.

As with most Huixcolotla artists, Ernesto started drawing when he began his apprenticeship at the age of 15. This is a tradition that perhaps derives from the original 16th-century European guild system which thrived in Puebla. Even today Poblano paper artists are considered "maestros." Ernesto keeps an impressive portfolio of his work, complete with mementos from dignitaries and celebrities who have commissioned his work or scheduled appearances by him in the United States and Europe.

The studio/residence of a papel picado artist is identified in Huixcolotla by confettilike scraps of colored tissue and mylar that litter the dirt street in front of the dwelling. Ernesto Vivanco's studio is also marked by a strand of plastic banners stretched across the facade, with "BIENVENIDAS" (welcome) cut into them. A generous, friendly man, Ernesto seems more interested in talking about his culture and art than in the tourist dollar. He says

Zapata Paper-Cut Out, ca. 1970s, Mexico, foil and paper, 20" × 16" (50 × 40 cm) 85.98G. The Nelson A. Rockefeller Collection of Mexican Folk Art, San Antonio Museum of Art

that many of the artists here are distantly related and form a sort of school. They take pride in the distinctive style and workmanship produced by their village, which is famous among connoisseurs for its papel picado.

One example of the Huixcolotla school is the blue foil *charro* by Florentino Vivanco Reyonosa, shown on page 26. His son, Florentino Reyonosa III, carries on the tradition as well. For all of these artists, picando is indeed a cottage industry, although their main livelihood is agricultural work. These artists, who have neither phones nor mail service, rely on middle-men—institutions and entrepreneurs—to take orders from tourists and art galleries for their work. The middlemen then receive a commission on the earnings. This arrangement connects the Huixcolotlans with a cosmopolitan art market that offers them opportunities far beyond their small village.

Where to Find Papel Picado in Mexico Today

You can find a wide assortment of paper picado designed by many different artists in Huixcolotla and Puebla in the state of Puebla, as well as in Mexico City, Uruapan, Oaxaca, San Miguel del Allende, Piedra Negras, and Juarez. The best times to purchase papel picado are during the celebrations for El Dia de los Muertos, Independence Day (September 16), and Christmas.

Basics

apel picado can be cut in a variety of methods; each has its advantages and leaves its unique mark on the finished piece. After reading this section, you may wish to experiment with some of these techniques to determine which method you find most effective.

Unlike other cut-paper artists around the world, Mexican artists generally do not cut their symmetrical designs on the fold. Instead they lay all of the layers of paper or plastic flat for cutting, except in unusually wide repetitive works. They work very fast, using one tool at a time, selecting the shapes in their design that tool can best execute. Then another tool is chosen and the same process is repeated with new shapes and sizes, until most of the tools have been used to realize the entire work. The artist works from small to

Tools & Techniques

HAMMER AND CHISEL

Mexican papel picado artists generally work with a small hammer and 50 or more steel chisels, each about five inches (13 cm) long. Each chisel has a slightly different shape or blade size. The tools are custom-made by Mexican metalsmiths, specifically for this profession. Intricate patterns are designed around the shapes their chisels can produce. A papel picado pattern calls for an assortment of sizes and shapes of chisel edges from tiny half circles to wide, shallow curves. Hole punches, needles, and leather punches are used for smaller circles. Larger holes are made by joining two semicircular chisel cuts.

A papel picado pattern calls for an assortment of sizes and shapes of chisel edges, some not much bigger than a dime.

large shapes and from the center out toward the border.

Woodworking chisels that you can purchase through mail-order catalogues or some hardware and art-supply stores are a good substitute for custom-made chisels. You will want to have most of the wooden handle sawed off, leaving about one or two inches (2.5 to 5 cm) to protect the steel.

When cutting the paper, the hammer needs to be as close to the cutting edge of the chisel as possible. This gives you more

Hammer and chisels used to cut a triangular plastic banner

control and therefore more precision in your cutting. You might start out with some basic curved and straight chisels and gradually build up a set ranging from $1/8$-inch-deep (3 mm) deep curves to 1 inch (2.5 cm) shallow curves. Straight chisels are the easiest to find in all sizes. A grinding machine is helpful in keeping the edges of the chisels sharp. Fine sandpaper can also be used, especially on the inside of the curved chisels, which cannot be sharpened by the machine.

PUNCHES

Hole punches designed for working with leather are recommended for cutting perfect holes of various sizes. These punches are inexpensive but wear out quickly from hammering. The paper holes tend to stay in the punches after hammering and eventually crack open

the punch. Picking out the paper regularly from the punch with a needle helps preserve them longer. Punches ranging from $1/16$ inch (1.5 mm) to $1/2$ inch (1.5 cm) in diameter can be purchased at hobby shops that carry leather-working products.

A mallet is another helpful product that can be purchased at a leather-craft shop. It is larger and easier to use than a hammer and is available in a variety of sizes. The heavier the mallet, the more pressure you will bring to bear on your chisels, and the more precise your cuts will be. However, if you are uncomfortable lifting the mallet repeatedly, it is too heavy. Choose one that you can grow into without discomfort to your neck and shoulders. Proper seat and table height will also affect your comfort with the mallet.

Example of a lead pad

LEAD PADS

In Huixcolotla, most of the chisel work is done on a table that has been covered with oil cloth, either indoors or outdoors, weather permitting. A flat circle of lead, about ¼ inch (6 mm) thick and eight inches (21 cm) in diameter, is placed on the table, and the stack of material to be chiseled is placed over the lead. The soft lead is kind to the chisels, preserving the sharp edges that have to be sharpened after frequent use. The lead also ensures that the bottom layers of the stack will receive as clean a cut as those on the top. How the Mexicans came to use lead for this unique purpose is a mystery. The heavy metal was being used extensively as early as the 16th century in glazing the Talavera pottery in Puebla.

The lead can be remelted in a cast iron skillet for resurfacing when it becomes too rough from the many chisel incisions. Do not try to do this in an aluminum pan. You will not want to use the skillet for cooking after it has become contaminated with lead. If you decide to try this on your own, take care not to breathe the lead fumes during melting. It is preferable to perform the task outdoors or in a well-ventilated, open room. Use a long disposable spoon or spatula to smooth over the surface of the lead and discard the residue that accumulates on the surface during melting. The pad will cool and harden in a couple of hours.

Either side of the lead can be used for your punching board; when one side becomes too rough and starts tearing your work, turn it over and use the fresh side. It helps to have a stronger paper, such as regular bond paper instead of tissue, on the bottom of the stack you are punching. Tissue can easily get caught and then torn by the grooves left by chisels in the lead pad. When not in use, cover the lead pad and store it away from children. Always wash your hands after working with the toxic metal.

INDONESIAN METHOD

On the Indonesian islands of Java and Bali, hammer and chisels are used to cut intricate shadow puppets called *wayang kulit* out of water buffalo hides. Instead of lead, a cross section of a tree trunk is used underneath the hide, just as you would use a butcher block. This method also works well for papel picado. In fact, having experimented with both, I cannot tell the difference in the quality of the cuts. A soft wood such as cottonwood works very well. I would recommend this technique as a nontoxic substitute for the lead pad.

CRAFT KNIFE

Cutting paper with a craft knife has the advantage of producing a limitless variety of delicate fluid lines and shapes. It is NOT for the very young. The technique requires strength, manual control, patience, and practice. Another advantage of the craft knife is the availability of the tool and replacement blades. Old blades can easily be removed and replaced with fresh sharp ones for easy cutting. Blade numbers 1 and 11 are the most flexible and universally used.

Small curves are the most challenging to execute with a craft knife, and you will quickly develop calluses where the fingers bear the most pressure. I use rubber finger guards on at least my index finger and thumb when doing a large cutting project with a craft knife. You can purchase finger guards at an office-supply store. Sometimes, instead of wearing guards, I apply adhesive bandage strips to the areas of my fingers that receive the most pressure.

To cut out a complete shape with a craft knife, you will have to overlap the knife cuts just enough to make a clean, removable shape. Be careful not to cut into the connectors that hold the whole design together. For best results, pull the blade toward you and away from the hand that holds the paper down. When cutting curves, it is sometimes easier to turn the paper, rather than the knife. A self-healing vinyl cutting surface helps keep knife blades sharp and your table surface unscarred. Cutting boards may be purchased at art- and office-supply stores.

Carmen Lomas Garza, a papel picado artist in California, cuts paper measuring nine by ten feet (2.7 by 3 m) using a standard craft knife. Although it is possible, it would be difficult to cut a work that size on a lead pad using chisels. The more flexible knife is preferable for cutting oversize, complicated works, because the cut shapes and lines are not as limited with the knife as with the chisel. A sharp knife can cut up to 20 layers of tissue paper at once. Cutting perfect curves, such as a scalloped border, is difficult and time-consuming with a knife but very easy with the chisel. I sometimes combine both techniques when working on fine art, oversized, or one-of-a kind works. Your cutting technique is enhanced by having the flexibility to use each tool's unique advantages where most appropriate.

SCISSOR CUTTING

Popularized by the European silhouette and the Chinese stencil, cutting paper with a scissors is the safest and most portable method. Scissor cutting works best when using small sheets of paper, which must be hand held and turned while being cut. A small pair of scissors with sharp pointed blades and large handles are most popular with professionals. For greater flexibility, you should have at least two pairs of scissors: a small pair for details and a large pair for outer borders and larger cut areas.

Five modest-size papel picado tissue banners, about 8 by 11 inches (21 by 28 cm) can easily be cut at once with good scissors. This technique is especially advantageous when working with symmetrical patterns—those which can be folded in half with both sides matching identically.

Such a pattern can be cut in half and attached to a stack of tissues, cut to the size of the pattern, and folded in half. The folded edge of the stack is then aligned with the center line (where the pattern was cut) and attached with pins, clips, or staples. Staples should be used only in the larger shapes that will be cut out, or the area outside of the border, which will be cut away last.

Cutting symmetrical patterns on the fold allows you to cut out the entire banner twice as fast. Symmetrical shapes within the pattern can be folded and cut (thus doubling the layers again) in the same way. However, sometimes with all of the doubling over, you may find that the layers have become too thick to cut. Once again, as with chisel and knife cutting, care must be taken *not* to cut through a connector, especially on the center fold.

When you want to enter an area in the center of the pattern to be cut, do not poke the pattern with the sharp end of the scissors. Instead, fold the area to be cut and make a small incision in the fold, while being careful not to cut outside of the removable shape. Then unfold and enter the incision with the scissors. If the area to be cut is too small to fold, as is the case often with miniatures, then there is no alternative but to carefully puncture the paper with the sharp end of the shears or use a small hole puncher.

Remarkable Artists Who Cut Paper with Scissors

Leopoldo Furlong

In the 19th century, Leopoldo Furlong, a German living in the city of Puebla, Mexico, made a name for himself by using a scissors to cut intricate bull-fighting scenes from a 1-inch (2.5 cm) piece of black mourning envelope. Furlong made his miniature

cuttings while at tea with a friend. He claimed it was good exercise for his eyes. Six of his works are found in the collection of the McAllen International Museum in South Texas. In a display case in the Casa de Alfenique in Puebla are 20 similar unsigned works, thought to be Fur-

long's. Although Mexicans are fond of miniature art, the citizens of Puebla are famous for their diminutive reproductions ranging from brooms to nativity scenes, all no more than an inch (2.5 cm) in height.

An interesting and mysterious coincidence has surfaced in the collection of 82 miniature silhouettes that are strikingly similar in theme and style to the Furlong works. The owner of the extensive collection, Mr. Howard Karman of Arizona, inherited the work from his father, E. M. Karman. The elder Karman, who collected the diminutive cut-outs during

World War I, recalled the artist as being of "Mexican-Indian descent." He said the artist held his scissors very close to his eyes as he quickly cut the elaborate paper scenes for pesos on a street in Mexico City. E. M. Karman identified the "master" as Jose Furlon. He also wrote a book about him that was never published and has since disappeared.

Some of these pieces are identical to work by Furlong, and one cannot help wonder if the two artists are the same man in different circumstances or two different individuals. Perhaps Furlon learned his skills from the older Furlong and

honed them to an uncanny resemblance. Mr. Karman's description matches that provided by another patron, Sr. Carlos R. Huerta, who pur-

Above, *Monumento a la Victoria* by Leopold Furlong; right, *Matador with Cape Facing Bull* by Furlong. Collection of the McAllen International Museum

chased miniatures identical to Furlon's from an artist dressed in traditional Charro attire. Mr. Huerta also noted that the artist, working with tiny scissors, was often seen in front of the National Cathedral in Mexico City. Some of those works have been displayed nearby at the famous Fonda Santa Anita Restaurant. These miniatures were admired by the Mexican muralist Diego Rivera for their extraordinary detail and animation. The artist sometimes cut the initials of his client underneath the art work to form a calligraphic "extension," or two-dimensional "pedestal", for the piece. The pedestal was formed by the white part of the envelope, and, just above it, the miniature silhouette emerged in contrasting black. The extension allowed the viewer to hold the tiny work by the pedestal and admire the piece at close range.

Many of the Furlong and/or Furlon miniatures deal with lively scenes of bull fighting and ranch life. Both artists cut almost identical scenes featuring a bicyclist waving a pair of scissors in the air.

Although little is known about Furlong or Furlon, their style is related to scherenschnitte, a form of silhouette popular around the 18th century, especially in Germany, Switzerland, and the Netherlands. Scherenschnitte is characterized by realistic detailed scenes. Miniature scherenschnitte scenes from the 19th century are included in a collection of the Museo Franz Mayer.

Full-length portraits in silhouette cut by a late 19th-century lawyer from Zacatecas provide further evidence of the influence of the European silhouette in Mexico. More than 200 of these revealing profiles of Zacatecas luminaries wearing top hats, canes, and tools of their professions, have been published. Each meticulously detailed study has been assigned a full name and title by their author. The parade of shadows conjures up an image of a hustling and bustling Victorian lifestyle in this thriving mining town in the middle of Mexico.

Victor Manuel Cuellar

An admirer of Furlong, Victor Manuel Cuellar of Puebla, uses a pair of barber's scissors to cut skeleton acrobats, ballerinas, and tiny pastoral scenes. The retired postal worker relies entirely on his photographic memory, rather than on his drawing skills, to create his images while cutting them. Although Cuellar does not make a habit of cutting miniatures of an inch (2.5 cm) or less, he has done some experi-

Above and opposite page, Three cut-paper works by Victor Manuel Cuellar, who is pictured on page 35 cutting the work shown above

mental efforts that are similar, but not as detailed, as the Furlong work.

For the most part, Cuellar cuts his humorous genre calaveras very quickly, sometimes on the fold. The result is often a figure and its mirror image attached at the center fold to create scenes that are usually no more than five inches (13 cm) high.

Franz Mayer Collection

We do not have firsthand accounts describing the cutting process for the diminutive cut-paper works in the Franz Mayer collection. All we know is that they were made in Mexico and that Mayer collected them and hung the elaborately framed miniatures in his Mexico City home.

When these miniatures are examined today, everyone is amazed that these works were hand-cut from paper. What tools and training could have gone into the execution of such treasures? The answer may be lost to history; however, the works of both Furlong and Cuellar are evidence that such works could have been cut with scissors.

This remarkable piece, measuring about 5" x 3" (13 x 7.5 cm), is an excellent example of cut-paper calligraphy. The words cut in script are hard to read, but the date, "1883" can be seen on one side. Museo Franz Mayer, Mexico City.

Materials

TISSUE PAPER

Tissue paper continues to be the most traditional material for papel picado, especially popular for indoor use. Its main advantages are the inexpensive cost, the quantities that can be cut at once, and the large and attractive range of colors that are available, especially in North America.

The fact that tissue paper is made in such a variety of beautiful hues and shades makes color one of the main decorative assets of papel picado. A traditional strand of papel picado usually includes a full spectrum—yellow, pink, green, turquoise, purple, white, red, and orange. In Christian and Buddhist cultures, white is associated with rebirth and is therefore used for altar and burial decorations, as is the custom in China. Although El Dia de los Muertos banners are made in all colors, the most traditional are white, black, and orange

(the color of the marigold blossoming throughout Mexico during this time). Hot pink is often substituted for orange, since orange is the color associated with Halloween, celebrated two days earlier, mainly north of the border.

When selecting colors for banner decorations, the setting or background should be taken into consideration. Traditionally, bright, bold colors will do much better than pastel shades in the open air and are the safest bet when you are not sure of the setting.

SPECIALTY PAPERS

New on the market are coated tissue papers, which are colored on one or both sides. Gold- and silver-coated papers are very attractive for achieving special effects. Specialty papers are also available with stripes, prints, and patterns. Striped and printed tissues will tend to confuse your cut work. Patterned paper is more effective with very simple paper cuts. These special tissue papers are usually twice the price of regular colored tissue. Their colors may be more permanent than the standard tissue colors, which fade with repeated exposure to sun or flourescent light.

Almost any paper can be punched with chisels or cut with scissors. However, some papers do not respond well to knife cutting. Coated papers and loosely woven or fibrous papers tend to tear under the knife. Amatl bark paper is very difficult to cut with a knife but works well with scissors. You may want to experiment with exotic marbled and rice papers and even gift-wrapping paper to achieve different effects in your paper cutting. Graduated-color papers also offer some interesting results when cut out and placed on a contrasting background.

BUTCHER PAPER

For oversized paper cuts, butcher paper is available in black, white, and an array of vivid colors. It can be purchased at reasonable prices by the yard from 48-inch-high (1.2 m)

rolls in most hobby and art-supply stores. Butcher paper is sturdy but not too thick for folding and cutting, and the colors are fairly permanent. Butcher paper and coated (colored on one side) papers make great cut-paper place mats. You can make a collection of place mats using traditional papel picado designs, each place mat in a different color.

PLASTIC

Because plastic does not respond well to regular glue, plastic banners are usually machine sewn to a plastic ribbon, sometimes by the artist himself. This is more labor intensive and therefore more expensive. The advantage is obviously a more weatherproof and therefore longer-lasting product. The Huixcolotla artists enjoy the higher prices, but the banners need to be replaced less often. From a distance, most plastic banners look like cut tissue paper.

You can purchase plastic in a wide range of colors and thicknesses at some wholesale florists and party-supply stores. It is most commonly used for table coverings and is sold in large rolls or folded in packages as tablecloths. It is an easy material to cut, although you cannot cut very many pieces of plastic at one time. The colors are fairly permanent, although the material tends to attract dust. Red, white, and green are the traditional colors used in Mexico for plastic garlands.

MYLAR

Mylar can be purchased in 18-inch (46 cm) and 24-inch (61 cm) sheets, either in rolls or folded up in bags. Many party-supply, stationery, and hobby shops carry mylar. It is available in a brilliant range of metallic colors. Although it is more expensive than paper or plastic, it is not as weather-resistant as plastic. I find it works better for indoor decorating, and I enjoy using it to make Christmas decorations. It is difficult to work with because the sheets are very slippery and tend to stick together. Putting layers of mylar between sheets of tissue and bond paper can help you handle the mylar more effectively. It also helps to staple the pattern to the mylar sheets as soon as possible, to prevent the mylar from slipping and sliding while you prepare and cut it.

Many retailers sell mylar folded and packaged. Unfortunately, once the mylar is folded, it stays creased; you will have to live with those creases in the finished work. The good news is that mylar banners can easily be glued to string or ribbon to make an impressive strand of banners that will not fade. Everyone will love them with or without creases.

In Huixcolotla, mylar is used mainly to make long ornamental ceiling hangings and garlands—elaborate fanlike snowflakes and stars—all of which are popular with tourists for Christmas decorations. These are more expensive, complicated works requiring some artful stapling to hold all the folds and cuts together. The many layers of mylar or plastic

Otomi pepper spirit figure

are laid flat over a lead pad and punched in the same manner as paper.

PAPER WEAVING

Mexican craftsmen weave colored ribbons and yarns into their garments, hats, scarves, and bags to give these items a flourish of color and texture. The same can be done with paper, or other materials, giving new dimensions to a simple pleated banner. The many scraps made while cutting a banner can later be used for collage on other art work. Long strips of contrasting colored paper or ribbon can be woven into simple geometric-cut shapes to produce an overall woven pattern. Ribbon and streamers may be woven through the side and bottom borders of a banner to dangle and float in the air for a festive effect.

Handling and Caring for Your Work

ELIMINATING CREASES AND FOLDS

After you have unfolded the finished cut-paper work, you can iron the paper to remove the fold lines and any creases. Place the flattened work between two layers of tissue paper and iron the lined or creased areas with a medium to hot setting. Do not use steam or water. Never iron mylar or plastic.

FRAMING AND PRESERVATION

When framing papel picado for use in interior design or an art exhibit, select a contrasting color paper for the background. The piece should be centered and attached to this backing at the top, then pressed flat between the glass (or clear acrylic plastic sheet) and backing. To attach the paper to the backing, you have the option of sewing, gluing, or taping (preferably with neutral pH, gummed linen tape) to the backing. This backing can be fabric, stiff paper, or mounting board.

To really show off the delicate qualities of papel picado, you can press the banner between two acrylic plastic sheets, inside a deep frame. This produces an elegant shadow effect on the wall, which, in effect, becomes the background. No tape or glue is needed, except at the top of the banner where it can be attached to one layer of clear acrylic plastic sheet. You can purchase the more expensive UV-protected acrylic plastic sheet from plastic-supply stores; it looks exactly like regular plastic, but will preserve the color of your work. Ideally, the wall behind the plastic will provide enough contrast to show off the color and design of the piece. With custom lighting, the shadow cast from the design onto the wall behind it will be even more dramatic.

If it is intended to last beyond a few months, colored tissue paper should never be hung in direct sunlight, high humidity, or fluorescent lighting. Only white will hold up as a cut-tissue window hanging. Mylar and plastic are light resistant and recommended as a substitute.

TRANSPORTING AND STORING

To transport a delicate cut-paper work to the place of installation, you can fold the strand up and lay the stacked banners between sheets of newspaper. The sheets of newspaper can then be carried flat, rolled up in more paper, or placed in a tube for carrying.

To store a strand of papel picado, fold it (accordion-style), forming a stack of banners one on top of the other, and wrap the stack flat in plastic or newspaper. It can then be stored away from sunlight and dampness. Long, oversize cutouts can be folded in half, if necessary, and separated with newspaper. Avoid using tape when storing and transporting cut tissues. Tape may easily catch and tear the delicate tissue paper connectors.

REPAIRS

To some extent, dirt can be removed with a little alcohol, and a small amount of matching spray paint can be applied to a discoloration. The most common problem with cut-tissue art is that it frequently becomes bunched and pleated—and this is when much of the tearing occurs. Fortunately, with some patience and care, this problem can be corrected by ironing. It helps to first gently flatten out the rumpled tissue; then press an uncut sheet of tissue paper over the area to be ironed.

When repairs are necessary to a torn paper cutout, mending with a minimum of tape is the easiest solution. The alternative would be to duplicate the damaged area by cutting the same shape from a similar paper, leaving overlapping connectors for gluing the new piece into place. This, of course, is time-consuming

and tedious work and is the very reason so much papel picado is simply destroyed when it is even slightly damaged.

Repairing papel picado is, in a traditional sense, a denial of its very creation as an ephemeral art. The fact is, however, that when possible, why not carefully fold the tissue-paper banner, and save it for next year?

MEXICAN WALL STENCILING
Sanctuary de Jesus Nazareno de Atotonilco

The sacred and profane are joined in a fascinating decorating project in the bar in the elegant Sierra Nevada Hotel in San Miguel del Allende, Mexico. The deep blue walls of the bar appear to be completely covered with white lace. In fact, the walls were stenciled in 1986 by a local artist, Sr. Lauro Almanza, to create this illusion. The Sierra Nevada Hotel manager explained that the hotel's owner commissioned an artist to reproduce the stencil work in a nearby church. The owner was very fond of the 18th-century Sanctuary de Jesus Nazareno de Atotonilco, about a half-hour drive from San Miguel.

Upon visiting the church, I almost missed the dark chapel with the original faux lace walls. It was at that time closed to the public. Fortunately, the priest was on hand to unlock the door and allow entrance. Indeed, here was the same motif and stunning effect, only there was more of it, and it was old and worn. The hotel manager had informed me that the three-dimensional illusion of white lace draped over the walls was achieved through the use of a stencil, (plastillo) and paint. The church dates back to the early 18th century, but I could find no information on the hidden chapel, which was distinctly different in ornamentation from the rest of the church. I have since learned from art restorer Mary Canales Jary that the pigment for the original stencil work was mixed with cactus juice, and that some restoration of the stenciling has recently been realized in the chapel.

Perhaps this is another example of an artist's effort to give the richest embellishment within his means to his village church. Not having the resources to purchase precious European lace, he used his talent and creativity to simulate the desired effect and with greater permanence. Sr. Almanza's replica of the chapel is an elegant and studied reproduction, as well as a tribute to the anonymous Atotonilco artist. It is ironic that, should the walls of the Atotonilco chapel ever be destroyed, we will have to visit a hotel bar to experience this liturgical masterpiece.

Projects

Pleated Banner

What You Need

▸ Tissue paper
▸ Small scissors with sharp blades
▸ Glue stick
▸ String

The simplest form of papel picado consists of cutting slits and simple shapes into a solid sheet of tissue paper. Banners cut in this way range from the pleated abstract design shown here to more complex folded snowflake patterns. Many Mexicans learn this method during their childhood and continue into adulthood the tradition of cutting their own paper banners with scissors.

What You Do

1. Fold a single sheet of paper back and forth (accordion style) widthwise.

2. Make cuts into both of the folded edges as if cutting simple paper dolls, leaving an inch (2.5 cm) uncut at the top for folding and stringing the banner. Motifs may range from simple geometric shapes of different sizes, such as diamonds, triangles, and circles, to more recognizable symbols, such as half-hearts and flowers, that are easy to cut from folds.

3. While the paper is pleated, you can cut the bottom border into scallops or triangles. You can also easily add a fringe border by making close parallel cuts along the bottom of the paper.

4. Unfold the paper; you may need to iron it to remove the pleat marks.

5. Start again with a second piece of paper. Try cutting different shapes. There are endless variations using this method, and I encourage you to experiment with different folding and cutting techniques.

6. Cut as many sheets of paper as you want. String them together as described in steps 10 and 11 on page 48.

Tissue Paper Banner with Two Doves

ere is the process, from design to stringing, to make a strand of papel picado. You can cut the banner with a craft knife and scissors, or you can use a hammer and chisels, as shown on page 56.

Strands of papel picado are usually hung from ceilings or in plazas or streets. Indoors, the strands can be stretched from wall to wall in parallel rows. A more complicated but stunning effect is created by crisscrossing the strands in rows perpendicular to each other. The third method is the maypole effect, where the strands radiate out from a central point. A chandelier might serve as the center, with the strings attached to the top of the fixture, stretching to the corners of the room first, and then to several other points between the corners. This is often done in church plazas, where the strands start from the front of the church and extend over the plaza to poles and trees to form a semicircular or fan pattern. A zigzag pattern or rows of parallel strands of papel picado are most often used over streets.

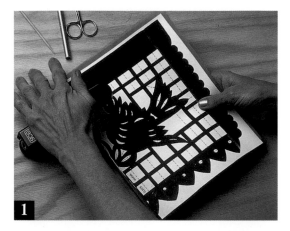

What You Need

▶ 5 sheets of tissue paper in colors of your choice, 8½ x 14 inches (21 x 35 cm)
▶ Paper clips or staples
▶ Small scissors with sharp blades
▶ Craft knife
▶ Hole punch
▶ Bamboo skewer or hat pin
▶ Hammer and chisels (optional)
▶ String
▶ Glue stick

What You Do

1. Enlarge the pattern (page 86) on a copier as indicated.

2. Fold the stack of tissue paper in half widthwise.

3. Place the pattern on top of the stack, match the center of the pattern with the fold of the tissues, and attach it with paper clips or staples. Never use tape, which would tear the paper (photo 1).

NOTE: You can use plastic, mylar, or foil instead of, or in addition to, paper. You will need less of any of these materials to make a banner.

4. Fold along the dotted lines and cut out the white shapes (photo 2).

5. Use the scissors to cut out the curved shapes (photo 3). Use the craft knife to cut out the white spaces within the grid (photo 4). Use the hole punch to cut out the small circles on the lower border (photo 5). Use the sharp point on the skewer to punch out the bird's eye (photo 6).

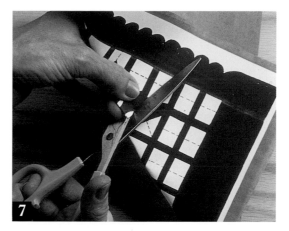

6. To cut the wing, fold the pattern and the paper, and use the scissors to cut out the shapes (photos 7 and 8).

7. Finish cutting the pattern, using the tools that work best for you.

8. Remove the pattern and unfold the paper (photo 9, page 48). Separate the sheets of cut tissue.

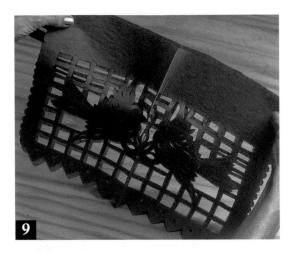

9. Iron the paper between two sheets of uncut tissue, using a hot setting (photo 10).

10. Now you are ready to attach the cut-paper sheets to a string to form a strand. Carefully separate the layers of cut tissue and place them on a large smooth, clean surface, or on a clean floor. Arrange the banners in a row, alternating patterns and colors.

This task is much simpler when stringing banners that are all the same color and design. However, if you have acquired banners of different designs and colors, the idea is to prevent any two banners of the same design or color from being adjacent to each other. Place light or bright colors next to darker or dull colors, until a lively, balanced arrangement is achieved. There should be at least an inch (2.5 cm) separating each banner from the one next to it. Cut enough string to span this arrangement, leaving at least a foot (1 m) of string at either end for installation.

11. Apply glue (a glue stick is preferable) about ½ inch (1.5 cm) from the top across each banner (photo 11). Gently fold the top of the tissue over the string, pressing the tissues together (photo 13). After all the tissues have been strung and left to dry for at least five minutes, the strand is ready to be hung.

NOTE: In Mexico, the artist who cuts the design does not necessarily do the stringing. Papel picado is often bought in quantities by a middleman for resale by the sheet, as a stack, or in strands. In order to make strands, several stacks of different patterns of the same size and theme will be purchased for stringing.

Patterns with Connectors

In order for cut-paper banners to be functional and hang gracefully in one piece, the whole pattern must be connected as if by one continuous line or grid. This calls for a network of connectors, linking each shape to the rest of the design. The style and organization of these connectors give the artwork its distinctive style.

The most common type of connector seen in papel picado is the grid, an overall geometric pattern that forms a backdrop—much like a lattice—into which the main design, motifs, and

borders are woven. The two most common grids in papel picado are the horizontal/vertical checkerboard grid, shown above, and the diagonal/diamond grid illustrated to the right.

These grids are best measured out in the drawing stage with triangles, rulers, and T-squares, making sure all the intersections are at right angles to each other. Keep the width of the connectors and the size of the squares consistent. Some of the squares can be left uncut to form a row of decorative squares or diamonds

within the overall grid. These grids are easier to cut with knives and chisels than with scissors because of the precision required to cut straight edges.

The diamond grid is a little more challenging than the checkerboard, especially if it is a symmetrical pattern. The easiest way to design your own diagonal grid for a symmetrical pattern is to first sketch the overall design, focusing only on one side of the symmetrical design. With a protractor, draw a connector line starting at the center fold and continuing at a 45-degree angle out to the side border. Make this a key connector where it is most needed to hold parts of the design together. Then begin making lines parallel to what you just drew, spacing them consistently from each other, until you run out of space.

Now overlay a second set of parallel connector lines at right angles to the first set, so that you cover half of the pattern with a diamond grid.

If you can eliminate connectors by enlarging or reducing motifs without compromising the design, seize the opportunity. The result may be a stronger, simpler (and easier-to-cut) pattern. Now trace the other side (the half which does not have a grid yet) by folding the paper on the center fold. Open and flatten the pattern. Check to see if the grid looks neat and forms a background for your motif. The grid should not call too much attention to itself. If it does, you probably need to check the angles of your connectors, or perhaps something in the design should be added or eliminated.

A third, somewhat more challenging connector, is an organic grid, such as the design shown below. Shapes and lines continually overlap in a meandering network of thin and thick lines. You will find the organic grid easier to cut with scissors than the diamond or checkerboard grids. Many examples of papel picado incorporate both the geometric grid and the organic connector system.

Organic grid of astonishing complexity and beauty, by the Mexican artist, Ortega.

Three Flowers with a Diamond Grid and Lizard with an Organic Grid

To experiment with these two connector systems, make tissue paper banners with one or both of the designs shown on this page.

What You Need

- 5 sheets of tissue paper in colors of your choice, 8½ x 14 inches (21 x 35)
- Paper clips
- Craft knife
- Small scissors with sharp blades
- String
- Glue Stick

What You Do

Follow steps 1 through 4 on page 46, and steps 10 and 11 on page 48.

(pattern on page 86)

(pattern on page 87)

Butterfly Banner

This pattern combines a horizontal and an organic grid to achieve a gorgeous design, as delicate and graceful as a butterfly. Echo the winged beauty's remarkable range of colors and textures by using several different specialty papers, strung together to form a strand of banners or a garland effect.

What You Need

▶ Tissue or other specialty paper
▶ Paper clips
▶ Small scissors with sharp blades
▶ Hole Punch
▶ Hammer and chisels (optional)
▶ String
▶ Glue stick

What You Do

1. Enlarge the pattern (page 87) on a copier.

2. Stack the paper; you can cut ten sheets of tissue paper at a time or half that many of a heavier paper.

3. Attach the pattern to the stack of tissue paper with paper clips.

4. Fold the paper and the pattern in half.

5. Cut the pattern, using the tools that work best for you.

6. Remove the pattern and unfold the paper. Separate the sheets of cut paper.

7. Iron the paper between two sheets of uncut tissue, using a hot setting.

8. Follow steps 10 and 11 on page 48 for stringing the banner. The design also works nicely cut from textured paper and framed.

This stunning snowflake pattern translates beautifully into a place mat. You can make a set of different colored place mats or stay with a single color. For an extra festive touch, weave thin contrasting colored ribbons in and out of the holes in the borders. Allow extra ribbon to hang from the lower corners and over the edge of the table.

Snowflake Place Mat with Woven Ribbon Borders

What You Need

- Butcher paper or other specialty papers
- Paper clips
- Small scissors with sharp blades
- Hole punch
- Thin, satin ribbons in complementary colors

What You Do

1. Enlarge the pattern (page 88) on a copier to the desired size.

2. Use paper clips to attach the pattern to one sheet of paper.

3. Fold the stack in half widthwise.

4. Cut out the design. Use the hole punch to create the holes in the border.

5. Repeat this process until you have cut as many place mats as you need.

6. Iron the place mats with a hot iron, if necessary.

7. Weave lengths of ribbon through the holes in the borders.

NOTE: For a more permanent table covering, you can have your place mats laminated. Two contrasting colored place mats can be placed back to back and off registered. In this way the two colors can be seen from either side, each dominating a different side. You will probably want to glue the two layers together and then laminate to preserve them. This technique adds color and complexity to your table.

Pinwheel Luminaria

Using the simple pleated method of folding and cutting paper, a standard lunch bag can be transformed into a festive candle holder, called a *luminaria*. The candle inside will shine through the cut work, casting a lively shadow pattern on the wall behind it.

Luminarias are popular outdoor decorations for Christmas, Halloween, and other celebrations throughout the southwest United States. About a week after Thanksgiving, white paper bags with sand and candles are placed along the San Antonio Riverwalk in Texas, for the annual Festival of the Luminarias. At night the view of the narrow river glowing with candlelight is breathtaking. The tradition dates back to Spanish missionaries who lit cedar boughs along roads to symbolize the illumination of the path to Bethlehem. Cut-paper luminarias appear to be a hybrid, combining two different Mexican folk arts—the punched metal candle holder and papel picado.

What You Need

- 5 x 9½ inch (13 x 24 cm) flat-bottomed brown lunch bag*
- Dry sand
- Glass votive holder
- Votive candle
- Paper clips
- Hammer and chisels
- Hole punch
- Small scissors with sharp blades

*White-coated and colored bags are available at stationery and party-supply stores.

What You Do

1. Flatten the bag completely by folding the bottom over and fastening it down with a paper clip so that you do not accidentally cut the bottom of the bag (photo 1).

2. Enlarge the pattern (page 91) on a copier as indicated.

3. Use clips to attach the pattern to one side of the bag (photo 2).

4. The pinwheel pattern can easily be cut with scissors by folding and cutting along the dotted lines. To cut this design, I used hammer and chisels and a hole punch (photos 3 and 4). Three bags can be cut at a time with

A SPECIAL NOTE ABOUT STENCILS

Many of the papel picado patterns included in this book, such as the luminaria pattern, can be adapted to stencils by cutting them out of water-resistant material. The stenciled effect would be a reverse of the paper cut, however, as you would be applying the pigment to the negative or open space of the paper cut. Any stencil design can be repeated in a row by registering the regular placement of the stencil to form a continuous border.

For multiple-color patterns, a different stencil will be needed for each color, unless the different colors are at least $1/2$ inch (1.5 cm) from each other in the stencil design. The pigments should be applied from light to dark. Oil or textile paint can be used on fabrics; acrylic or tempera paint work well on most other materials. The pigments should be used as dry as possible to prevent running or bleeding beyond the stencil outlines.

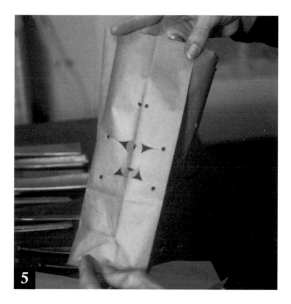

5. When you have completed cutting the pattern, remove it and open the bag. If your cut design stretches to the edges of the bag, you may be surprised and delighted to find a different cut design on the sides (photo 5).

6. Cut a simple scalloped border across the top of the bag or fold the top over as a simple reinforcing hem (photo 6).

7. Pour in about 2 inches (5 cm) of sand. Center the votive holder in the bottom. A long match is helpful in lighting the candle. You can also light the candle first and then place it in the bottom of the luminaria.

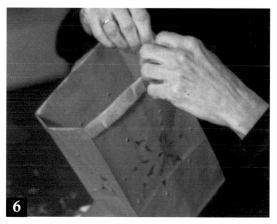

chisels; one at a time with scissors. Whatever tools you use, cut the design in the center or midway between the bottom and top of the bag. The idea is to hide the candle, but focus its illumination through the cut work.

(NOTE: You can create your own design and cut it out using a combination of scissors and hole punch. Simple shapes that can be cut on a fold work well in cutting paper bags with scissors.)

Hidden Heart Valentine

Simple lettering is often incorporated into the grid or background of a papel picado design, as this message of love illustrates. Lettering can even become a grid or connecting system in itself. Usually kept in simple rows and separate from the dominant motif, captions and announcements are designed to be readable but not confusing or distracting.

Use this pretty pattern to create custom valentine cards, or enlarge it and make a festive banner for a romance-themed party. The pattern features a symmetrical border that suggests a hidden heart. The heart can be left empty or decorated with your own message in writing or in cut work. This pattern provides an optional cut "love" message.

What You Need

▶ Sheets of tissue, rice, or bond paper in red, white, or buff

▶ Good-quality card stock in red, white, or buff

▶ Matching envelopes, red or red-lined

▶ Thin, satin ribbon in complementary color

▶ Paper clips

▶ Craft knife

▶ Small scissors with sharp blades

▶ Scalloped pinking shears (optional)

▶ Glue stick

▶ Pencil

What You Do

If you are enlarging the pattern (page 88) for a banner, please follow the directions for stringing a banner on page 48, steps 10 and 11. If you are using the pattern for a valentine greeting card, follow the procedure below.

1. Copy the pattern on a copier to the desired size. NOTE: You will find that the smaller you reduce the pattern, the more difficult it will be to cut. If you copy the pattern to fit a 6½ by 4-inch (16 x 10 cm) greeting card, you will find it easy to cut with scissors. Use a good pair of manicure scissors for some of the tiny curved shapes and a craft knife for the lettering. The scalloped border can be cut by following the pattern. You might also experiment with the various scalloped pinking shears now on the market; these can duplicate the delicate, clean curves that chisels produce.

2. Cut the sheets of paper the same size as the pattern. Stack the paper and fold it in half. Do not try to cut more than two or three sheets of paper at once, because the lettering makes it difficult to cut multiple sheets.

3. Use paper clips to attach the pattern to the stack of tissue paper.

4. The letters and the arrow (inside the dotted line) can be cut first or last. Cut them flat, rather than on the center fold; use a craft knife for best results. The shapes in the border can be folded down the center and easily cut with scissors.

5. After the cutting is completed, separate the sheets of paper, and press them flat with a hot iron.

6. Fold over the upper edge of the cutout as if you are stringing a banner.

7. Cut a 6- by 10-inch (15 x 25 cm) rectangle from the card stock and fold it in half. Make sure the cutout fits on the folded note card. You can attach the cutout to either the outside or the inside of the card. For a note card featuring a "mini banner" valentine, glue a thin red ribbon to the inside of the folded flap that you have made at the top of the cutout.

8. Now, decide whether to feature the cutout on the outside or inside of the card. If you attach the cutout on the inside, it will be better protected when it is removed from the envelope. Simply line up the top edge of the cutout with the inside fold of the card, and wrap the ribbon ends around the outside of the card, attaching the ends together either on top of the fold or in the upper back of the card. Make a bow, or overlap the ends of the ribbon, and attach to the back of the card with a sticker. If you don't want the mini-banner effect, you can also glue the cutout flat to the inside or outside of the card.

9. You can also cut a simple heart shape into the top of the card so that it features the "love" message on the inside. The recipient of the card will be surprised to open the card and find the larger cutout inside.

NOTE: This upper heart cutout must be registered perfectly over the inside cutout. To do this, make a tracing of the exact placement of the "love" in the inside flap. Lay the tracing over the upper flap so that the placement is the same as in the lower, (which it should be). Now draw the heart around the "love" without drawing it any larger than it has to be to see the word. Lay the upper flap flat over a cutting board and attach the drawing you have just made, registering the edges with your pattern. Cut the heart out of this flap with a craft knife following your drawing. Adjust the inside cutout if needed. You can sign it underneath the inside cutout or directly on it.

SAVE THOSE PAPER SCRAPS

Saving images cut from magazines, greeting cards, and sketches may trigger valuable inspiration. Scraps of interesting colored and textured papers, such as origami paper, shopping bags, catalogue covers, and gift wrapping paper, supply a variety of interesting materials. These scraps can be recycled into unique personal items such as stationery, little flags, book marks, and collages.

CUT-PAPER LETTERING

When incorporating lettering, you have two considerations: can you cut it, and once cut, can you still read it? In the hidden heart design pictured on page 58, a basic stencil lettering style is used for easy cutting. Even so, the lettering is the most challenging part of the whole design. This will always be the case. Cut-paper lettering is not a simple fold and cut procedure. It takes design ability and practice. Keep your lettering style simple and therefore readable. Cut only one or two sheets of paper at a time, using the sharpest scissors or knives available. Leave connectors within the letters, especially for complicated letters, such as the E. Otherwise, you will have flapping areas that are vulnerable to creases and tears, or that simply will not hold together.

This charming banner advertising an art gallery in Mexico City is an excellent example of cut-paper lettering.

Floral Pattern without a Grid

The active area in a design is what grabs your attention and dominates the design. Every design, including cut-paper works, must have both positive and negative areas to be interesting and pleasing to the eye. There are examples in this book of designs that use both the grid and solid background techniques within the same work; in other words, certain parts of the design have cutout shapes that dominate, while other areas use the cutout shapes as background for the cut-paper shapes.

In patterns that use grids to hold the design together, the grid and the elements they connect form the positive or more active area of the design. The cut shapes are the negative or less active spaces. Because there are no delicate connectors to cut in this pattern, it is easier to execute than the more complicated patterns with grids, such as those on page 51. As with the pleated pattern (page 44), you cut out simple shapes that form the design. Unlike a pattern with a grid for the background, these cut shapes are the positive elements of the design, even though they form holes in the paper. The negative area of the pattern is the solid, uncut paper that forms the background for the cutout motifs. This background connects all the cut shapes in the design.

What You Need

▸ 5 sheets of tissue paper in colors of your choice, 8½ by 14 inches (21 x 35 cm) or 1 sheet of butcher paper (for a place mat)
▸ Paper clips
▸ Small scissors with sharp blades
▸ Craft knife
▸ Glue stick
▸ String

What You Do

1. Enlarge the pattern (page 89) on a copier as indicated and clip it to the folded sheets of tissue paper.
2. Cut out the darkened shapes. Try cutting out the design using paper in two contrasting colors. Place the lighter colored banner on top of the darker one to create a shadow effect, as shown in the photo above.
3. String the banner as described in steps 10 and 11 on page 48.

Miniature Smiling Sun Flag

Small banners attached to sticks to make little flags, called *bandarillas*, are a familiar sight in Mexico for celebrating different occasions. Miniature banners are also used as stationery and business cards. These little flags add a festive touch to chandeliers, centerpieces, such as a bowl of fruit, and can even decorate a headdress. You can make these smiling sun flags quite easily and use them as party decorations or favors.

What You Need

▶ Sheets of tissue paper, 4 or more colors
▶ Paper clips
▶ Small scissors with sharp blades
▶ Craft knife
▶ ¼ inch (6 mm) wooden skewers, 12 inches (30 cm) long
▶ Glue stick

What You Do

1. Make a copy of the small sun pattern (page 89) and attach it to a stack of tissue paper with paper clips.

2. Cut out the pattern. You can cut most of the pattern on the center fold. However, the side borders are different, and you need to cut them separately, as one side must have an "extension" that you will glue later to the wooden skewer.

3. To make the decorative crowns that cap the flag poles, use the leftover scraps of colored tissue. From the scraps, cut strips measuring 2 by 4 inches (5 by 10 cm), as shown in photo 1 on page 64.

4. Layering three of these squares at a time, cut fringe halfway into each strip (photo 2, page 64).

5. Apply glue to the unfringed area of these strips (photo 3). Wrap three strips at a time tightly around the blunt end of the skewer, leaving the fringe above the stick (photo 4). Fluff the fringe to give the completed crown body (photo 5).

6. Apply glue to the extension side of the tissue-paper flag, and wrap it tightly around the stick, covering the bottom or unfringed area of the crown.

NOTE: If you like, you can enlarge the pattern to a banner-size and follow steps 10 and

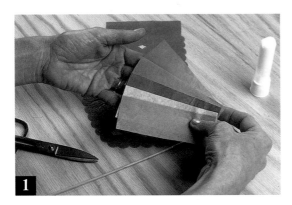

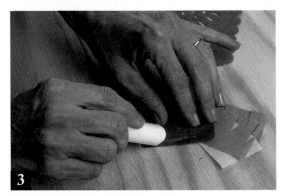

Cut-paper flags by Herminia Albarrán-Romero

11 on page 48 for making a banner. Or you can use the small version (without the side extension) as a bandarilla note card, following the instructions for the valentine card (page 58) and the Christmas Tree card (page 78).

Caiman Mask

This striking mask creates pop-up effects by folding triangular and rectangular shapes and only partially cutting them out. These projected shapes add texture and give the mask a three-dimensional effect. Pop-up shapes are most effective when cut from paper with some stiffness and body, such as butcher or wrapping paper.

The Caiman masked dance is performed in villages along rivers in the state of Guerrero. Caimans, which are similar to alligators, once lived in rivers throughout Mexico. The caiman mask may represent Xototl, the god of duality, monsters, and deformity. The pointy spines in this design are characteristic of this reptile.

You can make a banner, wall hanging, or mask with this pattern. For a banner, try using papers with contrasting colors on the opposite side to enhance the pop-up shapes. For a mask, experiment with papers that have unusual textures.

What You Need

- Specialty papers, medium-weight stock
- Decorative string, ribbon, or raffia
- Paper clips
- Small scissors with sharp blades

What You Do

1. Enlarge the pattern (page 90) as indicated.

2. Use paper clips to attach the pattern to several sheets of paper; how many you cut will depend on how thick the paper is.

3. Cut the pattern along the solid black lines and fold up the shapes on the dotted lines.

4. If you are making a mask or want to hang the piece from a wall or over a light sconce, thread decorative string, ribbon, or raffia through the slits on both the sides and knot the ends. If you are making a banner, glue string to the upper edge as with a standard banner.

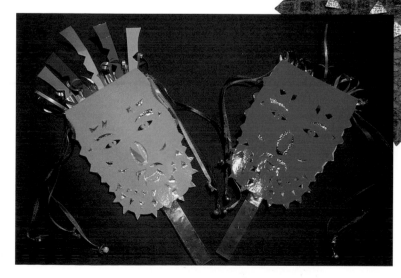

Cut-Paper Window Curtain

The delicate cuts in this pattern create a lacelike effect, and the rice paper gives the appearance of textured fabric. The project is based on a cut-paper curtain in Patzcuaro, Michoacan. It is a simple, easy- to-cut design derived from a traditional floral motif. You can customize the pattern to fit a window or door, and you can also use it as a stencil template for decorating a wall, floor, or piece of furniture.

What You Need

▸ Good-quality paper, such as white Japanese rice paper, large enough to cover the entire window*

▸ Paper clips

▸ Craft knife

▸ Small scissors with sharp blades

▸ Assorted chisels (optional)

▸ 1 rod, stick, dowel, or plastic batten for the top hem**

▸ 2 brackets and screws to hold the rod in place

▸ Bamboo skewers, 12 inches (30 cm) long to weight the bottom hem

▸ Glue stick

*Order a wide roll, at least 30" (75 cm) wide from a mail-order art supply company. If you have to piece together sections of paper with glue, the curtain will be vulnerable at the glued seams and will not last long.

**Any smooth, straight stick will do, but it should be thin and flat so the curtain will hang flush with the window. Plastic-supply stores can cut a clear, cut plastic batten to fit your window, and carry clear plastic brackets to hold the batten firmly to the door.

What You Do

1. The best way to use this pattern (page 90) as a curtain is to enlarge it on a copier to the appropriate width of your window. Then determine how many duplications of the enlarged pattern will be needed to cover the entire length of the window. That measurement will indicate how many times to fold the paper to produce the entire curtain. You might also experiment with tracings or copies of the pattern at different sizes to achieve a desired effect.

After calculating how large your paper curtain needs to be, add at least an additional 4 inches (10 cm) on top and 3 inches (7.5 cm) on the bottom for the hems. Now measure the entire height and width (side hems are not needed) for your curtain.

2. Neatly cut the paper to size. Use at least one of the manufactured edges of your paper for one of the outside border edges. Make sure the other side is the same distance from the first side from top to bottom. This will ensure a straight, perfect fit with your window.

3. Measure 4 inches (10 cm) from the top of the paper and fold horizontally over to form a flap for your upper hem.

4. Place the pattern on top of the hem and attach at that fold with paper clips.

5. The process for cutting the curtain is the same as for a fan-folded cut-paper banner (see page 44). Chisels, knives, or scissors can be used with this pattern. If you use chisels or knives, the only folds needed will be the overall horizontal fan-fold needed to duplicate the pattern. Begin the fan-folding process of folding back and forth horizontally, with each fold registered and pressed taut with the upper and lower edge of your pattern. If the folds are not lined up at the same place, there will be some guess work in the sizes of shapes you will be cutting from these folds. Also check to see that the sides of the curtain line up as you stack up the folds. You may have to repeat this process a couple of times until all of your folds agree perfectly with the pattern and each other. Continue folding back and forth until you have used all except the hem portion of your paper.

6. Finally fold the hem over at the last fold so that it also agrees with the pattern.

7. Using paper clips, attach the pattern to the folded stack of paper on all four sides. You are ready to begin cutting.

8. Begin cutting out the shapes in the center of the pattern. If you are using scissors and do not have too many folds to cut through already, you may be able to fold and cut all of the shapes on the inside of the pattern. If there are so many folds that your paper is now too thick to fold again and cut, then you may consider using a knife to cut the difficult areas. A combination of knife- and scissor-cutting may be your solution. Another option would

be to unfold some of the layers and cut fewer layers at a time, moving the pattern as needed. If you are using chisels, the entire pattern can be cut with one slightly curved chisel and a hole punch. No folding beyond the fan-folded stack is needed for chisel- or knife-cutting.

9. Cut out the shapes along the folded edges and remove the paper clips.

10. After unfolding the curtain, flatten each fold except the hem folds by placing tissue paper over the curtain and pressing with a hot iron.

11. Check again to make sure your curtain covers the entire window with the hems in place. Adjust the hem if needed and lay flat on the floor with the hem flaps facing up.

12. Insert your rods through the upper hem along the folds. At the bottom hem, a very light, thin stick should be inserted to help retain the flat shape of the curtain and add a little weight and support. Tape two bamboo skewers together at the sharp ends and insert them into the bottom hem along the folds.

13. Glue the top and bottom hem flaps to the curtain, leaving plenty of wiggle room for the sticks and rods. Apply weights, such as heavy books, over the glued areas, and leave for at least two hours.

14. Calculate where your two brackets should be screwed to the window, allowing some space between the curtain edges and the brackets. Once you have screwed the brackets in place, you are ready to insert the curtain rods and curtain into the brackets.

Mylar Hanging Ornament

This dazzling ornament comes to life when a breeze sets it dancing and light shows off its shimmering colors and folds.

What You Need

▶ 6 sheets of mylar in different colors
▶ Stapler and staples
▶ Needle and thread (optional)
▶ Craft knife
▶ Small scissors with sharp blades
▶ String

What You Do

1. Cut out five squares of mylar, each 8½ x 8½ inches (21 x 21 cm).

2. Enlarge the two patterns (page 91) on a copier as indicated, and cut them out. Both patterns should have ½-inch (1.5 cm) borders around them to leave room for stapling them to the mylar.

3. Staple or clip the top layer pattern to four of the five squares at the edges and inside the center square. Use five different colors, if possible.

4. Cut the four layers at the same time, folding and cutting on the fold lines for faster progress. Start with the center square; then cut the flowers. Stop there for now. Do not cut the border out yet.

5. Staple the bottom layer pattern to the fifth square, outside of the border only.

6. Line up all of the corners. The square hole should be centered over the dotted circle of the bottom pattern. Staple the bottom square to the other layers, again outside the border only.

7. Now cut the border out of the five layers at the same time, following the pattern on top. Separate the bottom layer from the other four.

8. From the sixth sheet of mylar, cut two strips, ¾ inch by 8 inches (2 by 20 cm). Lay one strip over the other at right angles to form a cross, as shown in the dotted line on the top layer pattern. To create the handle, staple the two strips together in the center (photo 1). For a more refined product, use a needle and thread, instead of a staple.

9. Staple or sew a 5-inch (13 cm) piece of string to the center of the handle (photo 2).

10. At A (as indicated on the top layer pattern), staple or sew the handle to the four corners of the top layer only (photo 3).

11. At B, staple or sew the top layer to the second layer between the flowers. Set aside.

3

4

18. Lift the string and watch your ornament unfold, revealing multicolored layers and flowers (photo 5). You may have to unravel and smooth out some of the folds and bottom slits.

5

13. At B, staple the third layer to the fourth layer. Set aside.

14. Use a paper clip to reattach the bottom layer pattern to the bottom layer, and, following the pattern, cut slits from the border up to the dotted line around the center.

15. Flatten the bottom layer out on top of the fourth layer, registering the corners of both layers.

16. At C, staple the bottom layer to the fourth layer only, at the corners, while pulling back the corners of the third layer. Set aside (photo 4).

17. Folding the top and bottom layers back, staple at D the second and third layer at the corners and farther in toward the center (two staples per corner, for a total of eight).

For a longer ornament, simply add layers, repeat the above process, and attach the bottom when you have achieved the desired length. The same pattern was used to cut the red, white, and green plastic ornament with many more layers that is shown on page 96.

To store your ornament, flatten it completely and place it in a plastic bag.

Faux Lace Table or Buffet Runner

This project is an elegant and simple way to dress up a dining room table or buffet. Vertical banners as long as 50 inches (1.3 m) are sometimes cut from two sheets of tissue that have been glued together. The thin glued line across the center is hardly noticeable after the design is cut. These oversize works are used as window hangings, or altar and table coverings. You can create a stunning table runner using this approach.

What You Need
- Butcher or lantern rice paper*
- Craft glue
- Paper clips
- Craft knife
- Small scissors with sharp blades
- Chisels (optional)
- Hole puncher

*Lantern rice paper can be purchased in rolls or long sheets 13 inches (33 cm) wide. You still may have to glue two sheets together in order to make the runner long enough to stretch across your table and hang over the edges.

What You Do

1. Enlarge the pattern (page 92) on a copier until the top and bottom dimensions are the width of a regular table runner (about 13 inches/33 cm).

2. Lay the pattern over one end of your paper. Begin fan-folding the paper back and forth, while lining up the folds with the edges of the pattern (see step 5 in the paper curtain project on page 69). Now you have an idea how long your paper needs to be. Cut and piece together the paper to fit your table and glue as needed. After the glue has completely dried, repeat the fan-folding until all of your paper is folded under the pattern. Make sure the two ends of your paper are aligned with

Similar to the shelf liner project (page 80), the table runner pattern is based on a fan-fold process with a repeating pattern. This pattern features a floral motif with simple diamond border inserts. You can substitute a scalloped border if you prefer. As with the paper curtain project, this design can also be used as a stencil pattern for a wall or floor border.

the edge of the pattern and the folds of the paper.

3. Attach the pattern to the folded paper with paper clips.

4. Cut everything out up to the area with a dotted line indicating "caution." The diamond borders can be cut easily on the fold as can the butterfly and flower petals. Use the hole puncher to cut out the many dots.

Before cutting out the flower beyond the dotted line, fold back the ends of the paper (these should be the bottom and top layers) and attach the "caution" floral section of the pattern only to the inner layers along the fold. The two end borders should not be attached to these inner layers. The "end border" pattern will be used instead to finish off the ends.

5. After you have cut out the inner layers, it is time to attach the end diamond border pattern to the ends of the paper. Make sure this pattern is aligned between the two long diamond borders you have just completed.

6. When you have cut out the entire piece, unfold the runner and press it flat with a hot iron. Remember to apply tissue paper between the iron and the cut paper before pressing.

Paper Doily

Cutting this lovely doily is similar to the fan-fold and snowflake procedure described on page 44. You can make it in any size and achieve very different looks, depending on the materials you choose. Use crisp white paper to imitate lacework, or create a contemporary effect with marbleized papers. Japanese rice paper with fibers running through it also works well with this project. However, any paper will do, including paper napkins. You might want to coordinate the colors of your table runner (page 74) with the doily colors. Paper doilies make nice gifts. Don't be disappointed if your friends place them on the window instead of on a platter!

What You Need

▸ Paper of your choice
▸ Paper clips
▸ Craft knife
▸ Small scissors with sharp blades

What You Do

1. Enlarge the pattern (page 91) on a copier to the desired size.

2. Take one sheet of square paper large enough to cover your tray or dish. Fold it in half and then in half again. You now have two folds. Line the pattern up to the those folds and the folded corner (which is the center of your doily).

3. Attach the pattern to the paper with paper clips at the corners and outer edges.

4. Begin folding and cutting out the white shapes along the dotted lines. Lastly, cut along the scalloped outer border.

NOTE: This is a basic pattern. You can experiment with more intricate patterns by using more folds and even recognizable motifs such as the butterflies in Cuellar Fernandez' snowflake page 35).

To make a stencil out of your snowflake design, cut the shapes out of the inside of the pattern only. Do not cut out the edges. Card stock or acetate will work better for stenciling.

Christmas Tree Card and Banner

Surprise the friends and family on your Christmas card list by sending them a holiday greeting made with this appealing pattern, embellished with metallic stars or distinctive ribbon. Cut the matching banner, and display it near your decorated Christmas tree.

What You Need

- Tissue or colored paper
- Good-quality, blank greeting cards in complementary colors
- Matching envelopes
- Gold and silver stick-on stars
- Colored string or ribbon
- Paper clips
- Small scissors with sharp blades
- Glue stick

What You Do

1. Copy the pattern (page 93) on a copier.

2. Stack five sheets of tissue paper or two sheets of heavier colored paper; cut the paper the same size as the pattern. Fold the stack in half widthwise.

3. Use paper clips to attach the pattern to the stack of paper.

4. Cut out the design.

5. Unfold the stack of paper, separate the sheets, and press flat with a hot iron.

6. Using the pattern on the outside of the card: Fold over the top edge of the cut paper and glue it to the front of the card. Position the gold and silver stars on the front of the card so that the metallic paper shows through some of

the holes in the cut paper, especially through the star at the top.

7. Using the pattern on the inside of the card: Cut an 18-inch (45 cm) piece of colored string or ribbon. Position the cut-paper pattern in the center of the string or ribbon. Fold the top edge of the tissue over the string or ribbon and glue. Place the paper pattern inside the blank greeting card. Wrap the ends of the string or ribbon around the fold in the card, and tie the ends with a bow in the front.

8. To make a banner, enlarge the pattern to the desired size. Follow the instructions for stringing a banner (page 48, steps 10 and 11), using the cutting tools of your choice.

CREATING YOUR OWN DESIGNS (Thinking Positive and Negative)

One way to begin developing your own designs for papel picado banners, stencils or stationery, is to start a clip file of motifs that might translate into simple black and white designs. The positive area is the more active area in the design; the negative area is simply the background or less active area. The cut shapes can be either positive or negative areas, depending on the overall design.

An important ingredient in the ambiance and charm of Mexico is the way merchandise is displayed. Everything from alluring arrangements of fresh fruit on a corner stand to elaborate candy displays in shop windows is designed with taste and panache. You will sometimes find these displays accented with paper cuts. Often, a colorful papel picado banner is used to cover a shelf, with the fanciful and scalloped borders hanging over the edge. The two patterns provided for this project are adapted from traditional Mexican papel picado borders.

Although shelf liners in Mexico are usually made of tissue paper, to cut these liners for your home you may want to use a more durable material, such as rice or gift wrapping paper. Fancy Oriental rice papers and Japanese lantern papers are thin, flexible, and easy to press after cutting. With these papers, as with tissue paper, you can cut into several folds with scissors to make one long repeating pattern. Experiment with different colored and textured papers to achieve dramatic contrasts and subtle lace effects.

Shelf Liners

You can cut your shelf liner as deep or shallow as needed. If you have a row of shelves you would like to enhance, it is best to use a slightly different pattern for each shelf so that you create visual interest. These shelf liners make delightful gifts for house warmings and weddings.

What You Need

▸ Durable paper or shelf-lining paper
▸ Paper clips
▸ Hammer and chisels
▸ Craft knife
▸ Small scissors with sharp blades

What You Do

1. Enlarge one or both of the patterns (page 94) on a copier as indicated.
2. Like the table runner (page 74) and the window curtain (page 68), the shelf liner is a fan-fold process. The longer your shelf, the more folds you will need to make in order to repeat the pattern to fit your dimensions. For a long shelf, glue two sheets of paper together, and let dry thoroughly before folding and cutting. Fold the paper as described in step 5 on page 69.
3. Attach the pattern to the folded paper with paper clips.
4. Cut everything out, using a knife, scissors, and/or chisels.
5. Remove the pattern, unfold the paper, and press with a hot iron.

Kissing Calaveras Shadow Banner

In Mexico, sweethearts give each other decorated candy skulls with their names on them as a token of affection during the celebration of El Dia de los Muertos on November 2nd. That tradition inspired this pattern, which is appropriate for use on that holiday, on All Souls' Day, or on Halloween.

For interesting shadow effects, you can glue a light-colored tissue background to a darker colored paper cut, as was done here. By facing the cut-paper side toward the light source, its shadow comes through the lighter background and creates an eerie ghost image.

What You Need

- Sheets of tissue paper in two colors, one dark and one light
- Paper clips
- Small scissors with sharp blades
- String
- Glue stick

What You Do

1. Enlarge the pattern (page 93) on a copier as indicated.

2. Use paper clips to attach the pattern to the stack of dark-colored paper.

3. Cut out the pattern.

4. Separate the sheets of cut tissue.

5. Reinforce each sheet by gluing it to an uncut piece of tissue in a contrasting color, cut the same size or slightly smaller. Glue the two layers of tissue together at the tip before attaching the string.

NOTE: A black cutout works well with a contrasting white tissue background. You will observe the "shadows" coming through the white "sheet." A quite different but equally dramatic effect is achieved by reversing the above and attaching a white cutout to a black background. To produce a luminous "stained glass" effect, try different contrasting color combinations. A slight breeze will add animation to the shadows as the row of banners flutters.

6. Follow the instructions on page 48 for stringing the banner.

Party Fun

When planning a party, design your own papel picado decorations around the theme and colors of the celebration. These can later be offered as favors to guests, who will be delighted with the souvenir. Wedding or baby showers might offer an opportunity for guests to help cut and string decorations for the coming events. Hospital rooms, front porches, and balconies can all be transformed into festive areas for celebrating a special occasion.

If you want friends and guests to cut out a design you created, first cut out the pattern yourself to test its durability, attractiveness, and level of cutting difficulty. Make revisions as needed until you are satisfied. This is especially necessary if you will be asking others, who are perhaps less experienced, to cut out your patterns.

Applying the pleated or snowflake methods to cut sections of an inexpensive paper or plastic table cloth for a lace effect will doubly delight guests and will help protect a cloth underneath. Even paper napkins can be transformed with simple cut borders. Matching doilies can be cut from paper napkins by using the snowflake method or other cutting techniques.

Patterns

Tissue Paper Banner
with Two Doves
enlarge 190%

Three Flowers with
a Diamond Grid
enlarge 250%

place on fold

FOLD

place on fold

fold and cut

86

Lizard with an Organic Grid
enlarge 200%

Butterfly Banner
enlarge 160%

place on fold

**Snowflake
Place Mat**
enlarge 200%

fold and cut

**Hidden Heart
Valentine**
enlarge 115% for
greeting card

enlarge 180% for a
banner

Caution! Cut unfolded, inside the dotted line.

LOVE

Optional: open and cut out lettering

Place on fold

fold and cut

Floral Pattern without a Grid
enlarge 120%

place on fold

Fold and cut on dotted lines

Smiling Sun Flag

enlarge 130% for bandarilla

enlarge 170% for banner and eliminate extension for stick

place on fold

Caiman Mask
enlarge 130%

Cut V's and fold back along dotted lines.

Fold and cut

Cut along solid lines.

place on fold

Window Curtain

Side edge / border

Place on fold

Place on fold

Side edge / border

Mylar Hanging Ornament enlarge 215%

cut four

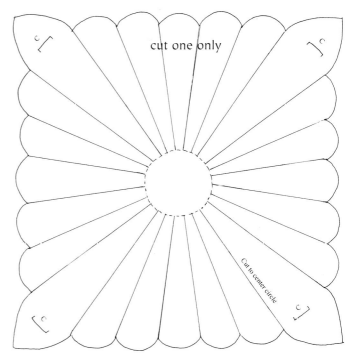

cut one only

Pinwheel Luminaria enlarge 165%

Paper Doily

place on fold

place on fold

Table Runner Pattern

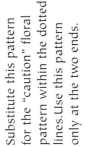

Substitute this pattern for the "caution" floral pattern within the dotted lines. Use this pattern only at the two ends.

top edge

floral pattern

CAUTION   CAUTION

bottom edge

place on fold AFTER pulline the two ends back.   end

Christmas Tree
Card or Banner

actual size for
greeting card

enlarge 180% for banner

place on fold

place on fold

Kissing Calaveras
Shadow Banner

enlarge 200%

Shelf Liners enlarge 115%

place on fold

place on fold

place on fold

place on fold

place on fold

94

Bibliography

Balland, *Diableries*. France: Imprimeries Aubin a Poitiers, 1978.

Berdecio, Roberto, and Stanley Appelbaum. *Posada's Popular Mexican Prints*. New York: Dover Publications, Inc., 1972.

Berliner, Nancy Zeng. *Chinese Folk Art*. New York: Little, Brown and Company Inc., 1986.

Carmichael, Elizabeth. *The Skeleton at the Feast*. University of Texas Press, 1992.

Cordry, Donald. *Mexican Masks*. The University of Texas Press, 1980.

Daoyi, Zhang. *The Art of Chinese Papercuts*. China: Foreign Language Press, 1989.

Garza, Carmen Lomas. *Papel Picado*. Arizona: Xicanindio Arts Coalition, Inc., 1984.

Gutierrez, Electra and Tonatiuk. "El Arte Popular de Mexico." Mexico: Artes de Mexico. pp. 98-99, 1960.

Jablonski, Ramona. *Chinese Cut-out Designs from Nature*. Maryland: Stemmer House Publishers, Inc., 1980.

Josephy, Marcia Reines. "Documents and Decorations: The Art of Jewish Papercutting," *Papercutting World*. p.10., Spring 1986.

Ledesma, Gabriel Fernandez. "Siluetas," *Forma, Revista de Artes Plasticas*. Mexico, pp. 253-270, 1928.

Padilla, Leonardo. "Maravillosas Miniaturas," *Claudia*. Mexico, pp. 84-86, June.

Sandstrom, Alan R. *Traditional Papermaking and Paper Cult Figures of Mexico*. University of Oklahoma Press, 1986.

Index